WHO'S CONTROLLING YOUR DESTINY?

# You've
## ∽ Been ∽
# Tweeked !

Bruce Lengeman

Tate Publishing *& Enterprises*

"You've Been Tweeked! : Who's Controlling Your Destiny?" by Bruce Lengeman

Copyright © 2006 by Bruce Lengeman. All rights reserved.

Published in the United States of America
by Tate Publishing, LLC
127 East Trade Center Terrace
Mustang, OK 73064
(888) 361-9473

Book design copyright © 2006 by Tate Publishing, LLC. All rights reserved.

ISBN: 1-5988643-7-8

# DEDICATION

This book could only be dedicated to my awesome wife, Ruthie, who, when there were no outlets for my writings, kept challenging me to "*Write, write, write. Someday God will open the doors.*" She also has been instrumental in helping me to uncover a host of tweekers that led to me getting set free in many areas of my life.

# TABLE OF CONTENTS:

# YOU'VE BEEN TWEEKED:

### REAL-LIFE AUTHOR'S INTRODUCTION

*You've Been Tweeked* is a bizarre story designed to teach a life-changing lesson.

It is about how you can defeat forces that have kept you from enjoying your full portion of joy, prosperity, health, love, success and more.

It is about the battle that wages inside you that determines

who you will become,

what you will do,

how you will live.

The setting of *You've Been Tweeked* is inside the mind of a normal, everyday guy named Elvin Greble. The characters are unreal, but the dynamics are as real as can be. This book does not contain the complete lesson in life that I would like to convey. I cannot write that. You must! For in this somewhat silly story, I have given you only an illustration of the war— the war YOU must uncover, the war YOU must fight, the war YOU must win if you are to reach your potential in life, or break your cycles of defeat.

If *You've Been Tweeked* is to change your life, the real work begins after the book has ended. Some of you may not have a clue, after reading this book, how it applies to you. *None of you will know*, upon completion of the book, HOW MUCH it applies to you.

Many of you who read this story will confess that you have been victimized by "tweekers," but few of you will know how. You have become accustomed to the subtle warriors fighting for your soul. They have become part of you. But now it is time to take control of your mind and BECOME AN OVERCOMER in life.

The story you are about to read is designed to change your core belief system—who you are, how you fit into life, how much potential you have, what you are worth, how valuable you are to others, what you accomplish and become in the future. It is designed to change your view of failure, people, self, circumstances, success and God.

## ◆◆◆ THE BROADER INFLUENCE ◆◆◆

Use *You've Been Tweeked* to teach your class or your own children how to move from being content with mediocrity to a lifestyle of *living to make a difference!* Use *You've Been Tweeked* as a catalyst for your small-group series in church, neighborhood chats, prison meetings, substance abuse groups or group counseling sessions. Do you know wayward teens? Depressed neighbors? Talented people squandering their life in poverty? Unhappy married couples? Food abusers? Discontented employees? Give them a copy of *You've Been Tweeked*, and then follow up!

Having not yet read this book you will not notice my subtle pun when I challenge you to read *You've Been Tweeked* with an open mind. My hope is that it will entertain you, but my greater hope is that it will radically change your life.

Get ready to declare war! Remember, Destiny Control is with you!

You WILL win! Write and tell me how *You've Been Tweeked* helped you!

# A WONDERFUL KEY TO LIFE:

## ❧ IMAGINARY AUTHOR'S INTRODUCTION ❧

My name is Irving MacDonald. This book is for those of you who are desperately seeking answers to perplexing questions you have about life.

You may call the mysterious experience I'm about to tell a supernatural phenomenon, or you may assume it was a dream. All I know is that it was very real to me, and because of it I'll never be the same. The way I relate to my wife, children, friends and coworkers has been forever changed. I expect that it will radically change your life, too.

Many have called me a wise man. Personally, I don't consider myself to be very wise. I am quite aware of how much I don't know. Nevertheless, people still come from near and far to seek my counsel in life. I know much more now, since this bizarre event, how to help people on the road to happiness and success.

If just ONE of the following is true, you need to seriously heed the message of my story:

If your dreams in life are not fulfilled,
If your marriage is failing,
If you live in poverty,
If failure follows you,
If you are confused about life,
If you can't say that you are genuinely happy,
If you have constant worries and fears that bother you,
If you are quick to get angry,
If you feel inadequate before The Creator,
If you are afraid to take risks,
If you fear change,
If you are depressed,
If you are controlled by what people think,
If you feel trapped living a life you know is not right.

What I am about to tell you is good news—wonderful news. I, accidentally or providentially, found a key that will unlock a wonderful doorway to the rest of your life. I trust you will not merely read about my experience, but that you will gain wisdom from it, and deeply search your heart and mind for ways you might benefit yourself and others.

# PART ONE: SCAM 101

## ⟨⟨ BRAIN FOG ⟩⟩

The night had been rather dark as I walked home. Fog had covered the path. I wasn't really able to pay attention to where I was going, for I was turning so many conflicting thoughts over and over again in my mind. There was no particular crisis pressing on me, but for reasons unknown to me at that time my mind was bombarded with so many memories, so many goals, and they crashed against one another until my mind was a kaleidoscope, with no single, solitary thought above the rest.

I had planned on spending a pleasant evening reading in the park to rejuvenate myself, but the book had lain open on my lap as I stared ahead trying to figure out my life, hardly noticing as night came on. Now, on my way home, I was frustrated, frustrated at the wasted time, the needless confusions—endlessly trying to organize my thoughts, my life. It seemed so necessary for some reason, but my mind just kept spinning in endless circles, going nowhere as if my thought life was being controlled by someone or something that I had no power over.

I wondered why I felt like I had to figure out my financial future in the next hour. Why did it seem so necessary to think over the mistakes of the past years? I had a pet frog when I was nine. His name was Winston. I let him out to play in the yard and accidentally ran over him with my bike. I hadn't seen him tucked away beneath the grass. I kept thinking about that— thinking how stupid I had been.

Had I changed at all since then?

Probably not!

Would I destroy everything in my life, just like I had crushed that frog? Would I keep encountering disappointments like I did then?

Why did that seem so true? God Almighty, why did it seem like this was the only way it could be?

## &#10086; DOORWAYS TO THE MIND &#10086;

The fog blew slowly by, vaguely revealing the road ahead. Suddenly I realized that there was a wall directly in front of me, and the path that led to a wooden door. The door was glowing slightly around its edges from the light behind. I had never seen this door before—it didn't belong on the way home, but for some reason it seemed as if it was supposed to be there, and afforded me no great confusion. Somewhat instinctively, I walked forward, seized the knob, and boldly opened the door.

Walking in I found myself in a rounded tunnel with soft, puffy sides and floor that gave almost like flesh. The walls and ceiling seemed to be transparent, but the dim light within the tunnel did not allow me to see what might be outside its walls.

Slowly I walked forward down the tube-like hall, noticing many corridors that turned off from the way I was on. Doors, as well, were plentiful, seemingly cut into the soft walls. Within a minute or so of my entrance into this strange tubular place, I encountered a prominent door behind which I could hear muffled sounds. Swelling with curiosity, I again boldly opened the door and entered.

I found myself in a small room full of equipment both strange and familiar—some looked vaguely like sound devices. There were microphones, boxes with buttons on shelves and stools, papers and instructions. And, sprawled everywhere in no apparent order, were small, thin round things. The room was overflowing with these things, some showing through half-opened drawers, some in disfigured crates, most in random stacks and piles.

The highest concentration of these plate-like things were strewn at the far end of the room, where a hunched figure stared ahead with an intense, frustrated look. He… or it, was a strange creature, with a wide, long nose, and hair on the cheeks that hung down in front of its knobby shoulders. It wore a simple robe, gray and frayed, and was crouching nervously, rather than sitting, on the large chair. Bouncing continuously in the chair, it stared intently at a screen sunk into the panel just inches in front of its face.

After a long pause it wheeled around and said, rather curtly in a raspy voice, "Oh, you're here! Stand there!"

He pointed to a spot near his chair and turned back again to the screen and announced, *"Elvin Greble's mind. I'm Crampz."*

## ⊛⊚ INTRODUCTION TO SCAM, INC. ⊚⊛

Speechless, I did as he had ordered and moved to the designated place. When he didn't acknowledge me further, I hesitantly questioned, "Where am I? What is happening here…*Crampz* did you say?"

"Can't you see I'm busy? Be patient a moment," he snapped. I waited a few moments while Crampz bounced in his chair and turned knobs and shuffled the round plates. Then he kicked back his chair and said, "Now, what do you want to know? But remember, it wasn't me who invited you."

Awkwardly I re-asked my initial questions: Where am I? What is happening? But before proceeding, and to avoid unnecessary details, let me just say that Crampz answered my questions, short and to the point. His answers, though, led to more questions. His rough-grain temperament made me feel as if I was dialoging with an angry badger, and though he answered each of my questions professionally and thoroughly, he did not elaborate, nor did he satisfy any unexpressed areas of my curiosity. I did, though, learn some incredible things about Crampz and the mysterious control room.

First, lest confusion set in, let me inform you that Crampz was expecting a visitor from *Scam, Inc.*, the boss organization. When I walked in, he assumed I was the one invited there by Scam, Inc., a new guy who needed the organization explained. I didn't figure this out until well into our conversation. Something inside me, though, cautioned me that I could not let Crampz know that *I* had not been invited to this interview.

Before I continue, should you have any doubts, I'll make it clear right now—*I am no friend to Crampz, his activities or his network organization!*

## ❧ TRAINING BEGINS ❧

Crampz began our interview by revealing to me his covert operations. And yes, I was indeed inside the mind of Elvin Greble, which explained the tubular hallway. The control room functioned in a remote part of the brain so that it could operate in total secrecy. *Elvin Greble knew nothing of this control room in his mind.*

"*Scam, Inc.*," Crampz informed me, "does not give much slack. They tell me what they want, and I better get results, or…" Crampz paused as if to find the right words, then simply said pungently, "or else!" The look of fearful despair communicated well to me the intensity of his situation.

"The best way to describe what happens here," Crampz explained and then paused, "is war—plain and simply, war."

"Who are you fighting?" I asked naively.

"Who?" Crampz repeated, and then sarcastically answered, "The enemy, of course! Who do you think we're fighting?" Then he calmed a bit and said in a disgusted tone, "We'll talk about those creeps later."

At this point in our conversation, I didn't realize that Crampz and *Scam, Inc.* are the enemy, at least *my* enemy, and certainly they were the enemy of Elvin Greble.

"By the way, don't you have a name?" asked Crampz brashly.

"My name is Irving MacDonald, but everyone just calls me Mack." I reached out to shake his hand, but Crampz ignored the gesture.

## ❧ CRAMPZ'S BACKGROUND ❧

During my interview, I learned some interesting things about Crampz. His first job was with *Warner Brothers*. He worked in the cartoon department. You've all seen those ancient cartoons depicting the struggle between good and evil that wages in all of our minds. A common scenario may be a cat that is looking at the fishy in the hallway tank. On one shoulder, out of nowhere, pops up a black-robed, horned, red-faced devil, equipped with a pitchfork, which begins to whisper in the cat's ear about the deliciousness of fish. About the time the cat is poised to pounce on the aquarium table for the kill, a white-robed angel, halo and all, pops up on the other shoulder to deter the evil suggestion of the devil. A war of influential words ensues in the subject's ears, which usually ends with the cat giving in to the black-robed entity. The cat learns his lesson the hard way by being ejected from the house to sleep under the porch. Well, that little black-robed devil was usually Crampz.

After about ten years of experience with *Warner Brothers*, Crampz was approached by a *big wig* in *Scam, Inc*. and offered his current position. If Crampz performed this job successfully, he would move up to overseeing the operations in multiple control rooms.

Crampz was very sinister looking. He certainly wasn't human. In fact, he still looked like a cartoon creature with three-dimensional attributes.

"My job is to make Mr. Greble a failure and to keep him unhappy, unproductive and confused, among other things," explained Crampz, "and simply destroy the creep's life!"

"But why?" I asked.

"*Control*, Dummy!" Crampz screamed. "There is no other reason. I and everyone else in *Scam, Inc*. MUST control, and the only way to control people is to keep them oppressed and disgusted with themselves and life. Contented people work their own purposes and the enemy's, not ours."

"Excuse me if I seem ignorant," I said, "but what do you have to gain by controlling people?"

Obviously irritated by my question, Crampz looked at me like I was an idiot from Mars and forcefully answered, "Because we want *THE POSITION!* Why else?"

I was afraid to ask what *The Position* was.

"But what…" I started to say.

Crampz interrupted, "What do these [Crampz pointed to the round plates] have to do with control?"

"Well…yeah."

"Everything." Crampz replied as he slid his chair back to the control table and grabbed a round plate off the shelf. "Let me show you how it works and then after my demonstration you can ask me questions."

As Crampz took me step-by-step through his operation I marveled…but I also grieved. Several times I had to hold back the tears. The longer Crampz talked the angrier I became. I was careful, though, not to let Crampz see my grief or my anger because I had already figured out that Crampz thought I was his unexpected visitor from *Scam, Inc.* I was careful to let him continue believing that.

## ❧ THE DEPTH OF DECEPTION ❧

"What we do here is block every pathway to peace in people. We do it by injecting negative and damaging thoughts and lies into people's *thought canals*. And that's where these tiny, round things come in. These are called *tweekers*. They're the latest in brain-wave technology. Their technical name is *Thought Wave Controlled Recording and Replay*. Taking the first letter of each word is TW-CRR—we call 'em tweekers. Each tweeker has a recorded message on it for replay that we use to *tweek* our victims' minds and alter the way they live.

No matter what good, positive or happy thought Mr. Greble can think, I have a tweeker that will counteract it. So, my job is to watch closely on the screen everything Greble does and thinks and be ready to interject the appropriate tweeker-message into his thought canal at precisely the right time."

I responded, "Oh, so this is what is happening to so many people in mental institutions who hear voices and think they're Napoleon or someone like that."

"No, no, no!" Crampz rudely reacted. "That's another department. I work with the everyday normal guy or gal. Not voices, *thoughts, thoughts*!" Crampz screamed, "*Understand?*"

"Ah…I'm not sure. Not to change the subject, but when do you sleep?" I asked.

"Since when do *Wartols* sleep?" Crampz retorted, then immediately continued his discourse. "We keep every move we make on video file for review, evaluation and to refine our techniques. Here, let me show you how it works."

He turned a few knobs and a clip of a child appeared on the screen. "This is Greble when he was a kid. His first dream was to be a social worker in third-world countries. Greble was not like most boys who dream of being a pro-sports athlete. Greble always wanted to help people—especially people in Africa. When Greble was with his friends, he was the nice guy who was always doing nifty things for others. Of course, when you're young, stuff like that invites ridicule. He didn't seem tough enough to some of his friends, and they let him know it.

"It wasn't long until we—by we I mean my supervisors and my predecessor—realized that Greble was headed toward becoming a real asset to the enemy, someone that stands *against* everything we stand *for*. So watch what we did."

Crampz turned up the volume and we watched the screen. "The voice that you will hear on the screen will either be Greble talking to someone or thinking," Crampz explained. "Greble is in his sixth-grade class and he just finished watching a video about the unfortunate people in Africa." Crampz hit the pause button. "Listen to what happens next. I'll play you two segments of the tweeker." Crampz hit the play button.

"Someday I'm going to go to those people and help them." Crampz immediately paused the movie.

"Wow!" I remarked. "That was Greble thinking!"

"Yep, and it was a dangerous thought. If some other kid had thought the same thought we might have let it go, knowing that he or she was just doing some childish dreaming. But not Greble. Obviously the enemy's design for Greble was to help people. So watch what we did."

Crampz hit the play button and Greble's thoughts continued: "…but I could never help those people. In fact, people don't even like me very much. I'm not even popular with the kids I know. Helping people like that takes people who are smarter than me and easier to love."

"Notice any difference between the first and the second tweeker?" Crampz asked.

"Well, one was positive and one was negative," I answered.

"Actually, there's more. The first was an original positive thought initiated by Greble himself. The second was a tweeker—a strategic tweeker played into Greble's thought canal to counteract his dream of helping the poor Africans. That's just one example of thousands of tweekers we use over and over again to keep Greble doing our will."

"OK," I asked, "But who records all these tweekers?"

"From time to time we'll make up tweekers ourselves, but mostly the tweekers are recorded directly from two sources: The first is what others have said to Greble, and the second, things Greble has said on his own—you know, self-talk. Whenever Greble gets his own negative thought we record it for playback at the appropriate time in the future.

For Greble, the best tweekers we have are from his father, his neighborhood friends, and a third-grade teacher. The tweeker you just heard was a recorded message of his father. Greble's dad often gets frustrated with him because he doesn't get better grades in school. One time he implied to Greble that he wasn't very smart, you know—he was trying to motivate him to do better. Another time his father asked him what was wrong with him that he didn't have more friends. We combined the two negative comments into a very effective tweeker. But the voice…"

I interrupted again, "The voice on the tweeker was Greble's voice, not his father's, right?"

"Right! I'll explain. We don't run an amateur organization around here, you know. We're slick and we're good at what we do," Crampz replied arrogantly. "We know that our tweekers are only effective when our victim thinks they came from his own original thought process.

"For example, if we played that last tweeker in the original voice of his father, Greble would think he was just remembering what his father said to him, and then he would be more apt to question whether or not the thought was truth. But when he thinks it's HIS thought, it automati-

27

cally becomes truth. See that processor on the top of the tweeker equipment?"

I looked in the direction Crampz pointed and saw the item to which he referred. It was a simple piece of equipment. There were several knobs on the front. The top had more knobs of different shapes and colors.

"That processor," Crampz continued, "takes any voice we play through it and changes the frequency of the voice so it sounds just like Greble. Now of course we do quite a bit of editing and switching around words to make the tweekers more convincing, and sometimes we even combine two tweekers from two different people into one tweeker. We have many slick tricks.

"For Greble, we have tweekers recorded—well, everything from Mom, to Pepsi commercials, from Doctor Clyde to Grandma Esther, from Mr. Crudge—the pee-wee football coach, to rock stars, and others too, but the voice that gets played back is Greble's voice. Pretty ingenious, huh?"

"Very," I answered.

"Let me play you some more tweekers," Crampz said.

Crampz swiveled his chair, pushed a button, and immediately the screen changed. A clip of Greble in his office talking with several business executives began to play. He looked like he was in his early thirties. It was obvious from the conversation that Greble was a business owner and the men in suits surrounding him were his management employees. After praising Greble on his successful decision-making, one of the executives suggested that Greble expand the business into neighboring states and gave a brief plan as to how he thought it would work, and why it would put their main competitor out of business.

"Now listen to this part," Crampz interjected.

"I don't have enough business expertise or personal charisma to handle that kind of expansion." Then the screen paused.

I was getting the hang of this mind game. Greble's mouth didn't move when those words were spoken, so I knew they must have been Greble thinking those words. Because the words were so negative, they obviously were not Greble's original thoughts, but a tweeker.

I confidently looked at Crampz and said, "OK, I think I got it. That was a tweeker, but Greble believed it was his own thoughts. It was probably the voice of his father again telling Greble that he isn't smart enough to do great things. Am I right, Crampz ol' boy?"

"You couldn't be more wrong!" Crampz replied with a chuckle. "That actually was Greble's original thought. Now I'll play my tweeker."

He pressed play and the tweeker played, "You can do it. You need to expand the business. If you don't grow bigger, you'll be out of business in two years and then you'll only be fit to work as a window clerk at *McDonalds*. Go for it!"

"OK, I'm confused now," I admitted. "What was your strategy there?"

"Crampz grew up thinking he was not qualified to fulfill his dream of being a humanitarian to the poor in Africa, so he decided—with my help, of course, to go into business. Actually, he figured if he could succeed in business, it would impress his father and peers and they would then give him the respect he desires and deserves. So my job was to make Greble a success in business."

"So his father would respect him?" I asked.

"Yes, of course," Crampz answered.

"But why do you want Greble's father and peers to respect him?"

"Because, Dummy, don't you understand? Greble will get respect for what he does, not for who he is. Greble knows how to do business, but that is not what he is designed by his Maker to do. He was designed to help poor people. The more Greble succeeds in business the more he feels good about himself, but only because of his success. His self esteem is wrapped up in his success in business and so…"

This time *I* interrupted, "And so he becomes a *driven* man who fears failure more than anything else and in so doing he sacrifices his marriage, his family and his true dream in life for the respect he gets from being successful in business."

"Presto!" Crampz shouted. "You're not so dumb after all!" Then he let out a sinister cackle.

## ✑ JOSHUA AND THE PREACHER ✑

"On this note, let me show you more." Crampz continued. "Everyone in *Scam, Inc.* works together and we all have access to everyone else's files. That way, when *our* victim is sleeping we can team up on someone who needs some extra attention. So let me show you a segment from Joshua Little's life."

We watched a few minutes of Joshua in a scene where he was handing out rations to remote tribes. Crampz played thoughts and tweekers, explaining them to me as he went. Crampz's tweekers encouraged Joshua to help the tribal people, but Joshua's original thoughts continually expressed the desire to be back home in the USA managing a restaurant. Crampz showed me this scene because it was opposite of Greble. Joshua had been designed by his Maker to be a successful businessman, but his pastor often told Joshua that simply running a business was not as valuable a calling in life as being a preacher or a missionary. The pastor used hard words to convince Joshua not to go into business and to go into missions. Tweekers of his pastor were often played back in Joshua's thought canal.

For years Joshua was unhappy doing mission work, but like Greble, Joshua thought that his worth as a person was because of what he did. He knew that if he ever went back home he would offend God and be punished. Joshua was never totally happy. He didn't even know what true happiness was. And because he wasn't happy, neither were his wife and children. Thanks to Scam, Inc., Joshua was wasting his life and forfeiting his joy by believing a lie, trying to please his pastor and God.

Crampz didn't care if Joshua helped a few people, for he knew that ultimately Joshua would self-destruct in his ventures and accomplish more good for Scam, Inc. than for humanity or for God.

"One person we encourage, the next we discourage.

31

It all depends on the circumstances. One person we make successful and another we keep poor. And don't think all negative thoughts come from us. No indeedy! People naturally come up with their own negative thoughts. We just supplement those thoughts when we need to. Often, once we get a good grip on somebody's thinking patterns, we can let them alone. They'll bomb out in life totally without us. It usually only takes us a couple of years playing our tweekers to our victims and then they're ours.

"Remember that cliché, *Sticks and stones will break my bones, but words will never hurt me*? The founder of *Scam, Inc.* originated that lie." Crampz began laughing hysterically. "That, my friend, is the biggest lie ever told." Crampz could hardly continue he was laughing so hard. After a moment of gathering himself, he calmed down. "Nothing in the universe hurts and destroys more effectively than hurtful words. Everything gets logged in the brain. We here at *Scam, Inc.* simply help our victims remember those words."

## ❧ MORE LIES, MORE VICTIMS ❧

As my dialog with Crampz continued, I was getting an incredible education. Often in my relationships with others I would see barriers that they just couldn't get over. No matter how hard I tried to encourage some people, they were simply not able to get out of their ruts. Now I knew what that barrier was—tweekers—that play in everybody's mind. These tweekers work something like an answering machine, but their messages are quite different. The various tweekers are triggered by certain actions or thoughts just like answering machine messages are triggered by the specific number called.

I knew that when I found my way back home, I must expose the secret control rooms active in people's minds—but Crampz must not find out that I was with his enemy. There was more I *must* find out.

"Crampz," I said, "tell me more about how you tweek people."

Immediately he responded: "We use all kinds of tweekers. The main recorders of the tweekers are

Parents,

Self,

Friends,

Society,

The media,

Entertainers,

People we respect."

"Do you have tweekers you use more than others?" I asked.

"Oh my, yes! I'll give you some examples of popular tweekers I use to destroy people:

'You're a bad girl!'

'You're too ugly to be successful!'

'Everything you do is sloppy!'

'If people see who you really are they won't like you!'

'Don't try that because you'll fail!'

'You aren't good enough to make God happy with you!'

33

'You need to have a little fun before you get
serious in life!'
'No matter how hard you try you'll never be as
good as your sister!'
'If you fail at this you'll be a nobody!'
'You have to look good and be in shape to be
socially acceptable!'
'Making money is the only way to get ahead!'
'It's better to be poor than affluent!'
'You don't have the ability to do this!'
'If you put your fellow workers down, you'll
get ahead!'"

## ❦ MORE GRUELING DETAILS ❦

Crampz then told me some stories of cases he has
worked on.

"Janet had a great relationship with a guy in college.
They were engaged to be married. One day she saw him
holding hands with one of her girlfriends. She immediately
ended the engagement. Janet never had another long-last-
ing relationship with a guy because the tweekers kept telling her that she was just setting herself up to be hurt again.
That tweeker was a *playback* of her mom's reaction when,
shortly after the breakup, Janet called home to tell her mom
that she had met another great guy. We played back that
tweeker hundreds of times in her mind: 'You're just setting
yourself up to be hurt again. You're just setting yourself up
to be hurt again.'

"Fear and jealousy entered into her relationships and

always destroyed them. The truth is that Janet could have had a great marriage." Crampz again started laughing hysterically, "None of the guys she dated would have ever ditched her like that first creep. But she listened over and over again to that wonderful lie her mom recorded for us.

"Then there was Dave. Stupid old Dave. He believed us time and time again. Actually, we didn't have to use many tweekers to destroy Dave's destiny. He had this brother that was into cars and mechanics. Dave was into reading and poetry. He loved playing chess. He was absolutely in the dark when it came to cars and mechanics. His older brother would constantly call him a *prissy sissy* because he couldn't handle himself in the garage. *Poetry*, his brother always told him, *is for girls*.

"Dave grew up thinking himself to be less of a man because of the cruel words of his brother. We played his brother's tweekers on a regular basis. The truth is that Dave wasted half of his youth trying to find his identity as a man by lifting weights. He tried to impress people with his driving, and would drive fast and buy hot cars, but he ended up losing his license because he had too many accidents. That only made the situation worse. Hah! Dave would have been an awesome English teacher had we let him alone. Instead, his poor self-image ruined his marriage and his life.

"We have certain standard techniques that work to destroy people. We already talked about one of the biggest— getting people to find their identity in what they do instead of who they are. People who aren't secure in who they are live their life trying to impress people—and our tweekers to perpetuate this in their minds are a dime a dozen.

"Another one of the basics in our business is to destroy people's confidence. People who are confident—or have faith, can do most anything they want to do, so we are constantly working to destroy confidence.

"Shame and regret is another effective technique. All we do is remind people continually of all their failures, the stupid things they did growing up, their embarrassing and shameful experiences and all the wrong choices that resulted in lost opportunities. The goal is to drive them into a *safety zone* of behavior where they don't try anything that might cause them additional regret. In so doing, we render them virtually worthless to the enemy, and they become extremely focused on self.

"Most everyone believes that happiness and success are dependent upon circumstances, but are they ever wrong. Happiness and success has nothing to do with circumstances, but with the attitude in the mind. If people think they are at the mercy of circumstances, they will live life underneath the control of circumstances, but if people think they can overcome circumstances, they always will. We keep people believing the lie—*circumstances are all-powerful.*

"We also have auto-play tweekers. These are tweekers that go off every couple of hours automatically. These lies are so ingrained in a person's psyche that they have no clue they're being controlled by these tweekers.

"Celia was one of those cases. A brother sexually abused her when she was young. We put an auto-tweeker in her psyche that told her if she was ugly no guy would want to abuse her again sexually. Outside she wanted to be beautiful, but inside she ran from the pain of the abuse and subconsciously became hideously ugly. She was right." Crampz belly-laughed again, "No guy wanted her.

"Kim ruined her marriage, thanks to me, because I tapped in on her insecurity. Her dad never expressed love to her. No matter what she did she couldn't get her dad's attention. I kept on playing tweekers her dad recorded for me, tweekers that made her desire for the security of her husband's love more than any human could ever provide. She was so easy to offend. Her husband finally gave up and left her and the kids.

"Jeff, another idiot, was sicker than a dog with every kind of disease most of his life, thanks to me."

"What?" I said. "What does sickness have to do with tweekers?"

"Oh man, are you from another planet or what?" Crampz said. "Crush a man's mind, make him forget his dreams, push him till he's stressed to the max, make him a slave of what people think, and you upset the whole pattern of healthy living, including the body. People who are off track in life are usually sick, sick people. And no medicine will change that. If we can keep people oppressed with their thoughts, guaranteed they'll get sick."

## ❧ DOMINATING-PATTERN WARFARE ❧

"What are those larger-sized tweekers over there?" I asked, pointing to a large, messy stack of large round plates.

"Those are our most important tools—pattern plates.

37

They in some senses are the background format for everything else. In simple terms, these are generic comments that are formatted in cooperative packages that create a distinctive pattern of thinking."

"Am I supposed to understand what that means?" I snapped.

"Oh, yeah, I forgot I'm talking to a dummy!" Crampz replied without a single ray of warmth. "A pattern plate," he continued, "is a package—emphasis—*a package*, of mind-infiltration injections that run continuously, like as in *ALL THE TIME*, in the victim's subconscious. These package deals influence the victim's personality. For example, here," he paused to scavenge through a disorderly pile, "is a pattern plate called *Control Before Being Controlled*. Here's another one called *Comply For Peace*. This one is *Not Worthy of Love*. Here's one called *Run From Conflict*, and another, *Fear of Rejection*. We've got zillions of these *pattern plates*."

Crampz continued, "If you're familiar with computer viruses, you'll understand pattern plates. Viruses infect computers by running secretly in the background while disrupting the computer's operation. Pattern plates are mind viruses that are constantly disrupting the victim's choices, behavior, motives and reactions. They are incredibly damaging. Most people know something is wrong with themselves underneath the surface, but few ever detect our masterful *pattern* tweakers. Pattern plates define the core of a person's personality."

Surprisingly enough, Crampz continued with his explanation. I could tell it wasn't because he was liking me better, but it was because he was so thrilled with this process of deceiving people: "For example, you've met insecure people who second guess everything they say and do. That's because in the background of their mind is our *PLOM*, that stands for *Poor Little Old Me*, virus.

At that I injected, "And these are nothing more than an overriding library of lies!"

"Oh man, you ARE stupid! Like, mega-deficient! *Why would we just tell lies, Dummy?*"

"Wait a minute! Everything you do is based on lies!" I responded.

"Yeah, lies are part of it all, but pattern plates would never work if we just told lies. The bondage is in what is TRUE. Understand? Of course you don't." Then he mumbled under his breath as he reached for another plate, "How can I expect a novice creep to understand brilliance."

"Okay, it's like this—we ALWAYS are lying—I mean ALWAYS, but most of what we say is true."

"I may be a dummy, but that statement is about as oxymoronic as any I've ever heard. You lie by telling the truth?"

"That's exactly right. Would you like to pat me on the back now or later?" Crampz said with a cocky sneer.

"Go on," I said.

"Take this here pattern plate called *Domination of Past Failures*. This, my friend," he paused, then added, "my creep friend, is how half the world defines themselves—according to past mistakes. Why? 'Cause of us. There's not one solitary tweeker on this plate that tweeks something that isn't true. It's a revolving virus, tweeking in the subconscious, morning, noon and night. We inject it once, and it never quits."

Crampz stopped and placed the pattern plate on his desk. I waited a short moments until I realized—Crampz was already finished with his explanation. At that I exclaimed, "That's all you're going to tell me? What's so dangerous about true things?"

"If you insist. I'll play it for you. This is a pattern plate we tweeked for a guy who got too self-confidant. He ended up losing his business, his family and friends. He would love to try again, but unfortunately, for him, not us, our *Failure* pattern plate keeps him living in the domination of his past. Now listen."

Crampz skipped quickly through the package of signals:

"You failed more times than anyone in your family."

"You've got an incredible amount of work to do to undo what you've done."

"There's a chance you may fail again."

"Some people won't forgive you for what you've done, and will hold that against you if you try again."

"Choosing to do something safer and with less risk will be a much better guarantee that you won't fail again."

"Accepting the fact that you are a failure will be easier than trying to rise above your past."

"Your failure was because of your own selfish independence."

Crampz explained, "Everything you heard is true—yet they're all lies."

I responded, "*That* you don't have to explain to me. I

understand now. Though these tweekers are true, it's not the WHOLE truth, right? Like the law of aerodynamics supercedes gravity, there are OTHER *pattern plates* that would help your victim make a comeback in life and get back living successfully. Now I get it! Those superceding plates are in the enemy's possession. Let me guess the names of some of them: *Courage After Failure*, or *I Was Made to Be An Overcomer*."

"Don't mention those plates! They give me hives!"

I continued my discourse of understanding: "Like, I guess it IS true that taking the safer route is a better guarantee of not failing again, but what you don't tell him is the other half of the truth, that he will never be fulfilled by taking the safe route. You make him feel ashamed by telling him that his failure was because of his own selfish independence, but you don't tell him that he can ask forgiveness to those he hurt and start fresh with a better attitude.

"You tell him that many people will never forgive him, and you get him focusing on this TRUE SIGNAL, but you don't tell him that most people WILL forgive him, and those who don't forgive him will likely not hinder him in any way.

"You tell him that he has failed more than any of his siblings, yet you don't tell him that he still has plenty of time to undo the mistakes and succeed as much as anyone in his family. I get it!"

"Right you are," affirmed Crampz very meekly. Then he added, "Not bad for an imbecile."

I then asked Crampz, "But what happens to those individuals who somehow detect this packaged mind virus?"

41

"That is one of our most dangerous threats. Crampz answered. We have to protect our victims from other people who have enough love for our victim to expose their viruses. Our victims rarely detect these patterns themselves, but friends, spouses and counselors often point them out. And if they do, and the victims *perceive it inside themselves*, they can get free from the grip of the whole style package all at once. Usually when this happens, we never get them back, at least in that area."

Suddenly the light bulb went off in my brain again, "So my childhood friend, Jonnie Stewart, who was *always* down on himself…he had *PLOM* pattern plate controlling his personality."

"Yep." Crampz agreed with a smirk.

"And Jessica Smeldon, who never got close to anyone, she had the…"

Crampz interrupted, "…the *People Will Always Hurt You* plate."

"And I guess it's true," I said, "People close to you will eventually hurt you in some way, but the real truth is that love overcomes those hurts…right?"

"You sound disgusting. Like you're working for THEM."

## ❧ MACK'S REVELATION ❧

Suddenly something dawned on me. I tuned out Crampz in order to process a great revelation I was receiving—the confusion at the park—the negative memories on the walk home…and Winston—that's why I was so oppressed by what I had done to Winston. Winston was just a frog, yet Scam, Inc. had used the accident on the bike to make me feel stupid and evil, as if I was a murderer for running over him. A flood of past incidents of depression and confusion invaded my mind. It was *Scam, Inc.* These wiley creatures had guided me right into my present state of despair. Now it was making sense. Time and again I had believed the lies that flooded my mind—and I let it happen. Now I was indignant, I was horrified, yet beneath the anger I was elated with joy. *Scam Inc.* had just been exposed in my own mind and never again would I allow those silly lies to keep me from who I was designed to be. I was brought into this control room for a purpose, and suddenly I felt alive in a new way. I felt as if I had just become a warrior bitterly determined to crush the enemy.

A few minutes later, I tuned my attention back into Crampz who was still fluently exposing his diabolical strategy:

"Of course, nothing ruins people like holding grudges. If we can keep people from forgiving those who have wronged them, they're ours.

"Oh, I almost left out one of our biggest selection of tweekers, the *shoulda-oughtas*."

"The *WHAT*?" I asked.

"The *shoulda-oughtas*. Tweekers in this category are easy to get, and they're as effective as any other kind of tweeker. They're so plentiful we don't use ¼ of them. From birth to death, the people our victims respect are telling them what they should-ought to do. Parents and preachers, presidents and peers, teachers and bosses, TV talk-show

43

hosts—everybody has an idea what someone else should-ought to do.

"I figure there are more people on antidepressants because of our shoulda-oughtas than any other kind of tweeker we play. And the thing is: most of these people are the good people who really care about doing right. That's why these tweekers are so effective—and they destroy the people with the best hearts.

"We have moms running everywhere for their kids, volunteering in community projects, going to church functions—stressed out to the max. We got men taking all sorts of courses to get ahead while working overtime in order to be a good provider—literally sucking the life out of everyone around them. We keep people running from one task to the other, while leaving the really important things in the dust. And all we have to do is replay their own personal *shoulda-oughta* tweekers, knowing that people are dumb enough to believe them. Who knows how to live a quiet and peaceable life anymore?" Crampz screamed in pride. "You can thank me later," he finished facetiously.

"Simply, nobody measures up. Everyone is behind, or short of their goals. The results: doctor visits, broken families, drugs, alcohol, pornography, gluttony, and, not to mention, points for Scam, Inc..

"Did I mention *image* tweekers? We have thousands of professionals making these tweekers for us."

"You mean at *Scam, Inc.*?" I asked.

"No dummy! At advertisement firms, in Hollywood—you know, commercials, movies, TV sitcoms, talk shows, billboards, catalogs—all telling YOU what YOU need to look like, all telling YOU how YOU can be accepted in society.

If you don't have this kind of car,

If you don't eat at this restaurant,

If you don't have this kind of shape,

If you don't wear this kind of clothing,

If you don't drink this kind of beer,

If you are not politically correct— then you are not acceptable. These are all a bunch of lies we use to keep people striving to measure up to an image that someone else has created for them. Simply, these influencers make their money by deceiving naïve humans. Who cares what celebrity eats hamburgers at McDonald's, or who drinks a Pepsi? Ha, ha! Everyone does...well, almost everyone."

I gasped and said, "It seems so unbelievable."

"It is to you, Macky," Crampz said, "Because you're here and you see what's happening. That's why the worst thing that can happen to us is for people to find out about us. Exposure is just short of the guillotine in our business.

"Tweekers," he explained, "are a big part of the reason why people become Olympic champions, and tweekers are why people who could be Olympic champions never even make it to the Olympic trials. Tweekers are why some people fail in business, marriage and life, and tweekers are why some succeed in these areas. Tweekers are why intelligent or creative people never prosper in anything they do, and tweekers are why less intelligent or less creative people excel. Tweekers are why some people will never be happy, and tweekers are why some people will never live in despair."

"Wait a minute," I exclaimed. "Did I just hear you say that sometimes you DO make people happy, and help people to excel in a good way?"

"Dummy! Did I say that?" Crampz replied angrily. "I said, *TWEEKERS* are why people will never be happy, and *TWEEKERS* are why people will never be unhappy. I said *TWEEKERS* help people succeed in marriage and *TWEEKERS* help people succeed in life."

"What do you mean?"

"Here, let me show you two more videos." Crampz turned a few more knobs and in a few moments was ready to go. "Watch this," he said.

## ❧ THE ENEMY UNVEILED ☙

Back on the screen, to my surprise was Greble. Greble was handing out rations to tribal people. He was obviously a bit older than he was in the first clips. Crampz switched to another tweeker, and there was Joshua Little greeting people as they came into a restaurant. His wife was the hostess. She had a bright glow surrounding her countenance, and smiled warmly to her husband when they caught each other's eye.

"What is going on here?" I said as I shook my head in confusion. "I thought I was just starting to figure this thing out."

"You indeed are stupid," Crampz mumbled angrily under his breath as he turned a few more knobs. He obviously was not designed for public-relations work.

"Don't you understand?" Crampz looked at me and

screamed. I could tell there was something that Crampz didn't want to talk about.

"Dummy! There's another side to this! We're not the only guys playing tweekers!"

"Ohhhh," I said passionately. Suddenly I felt like a dummy. Of course: "The enemy!" I shouted.

"Riiiiiiiiiiiight!" Crampz said sarcastically. Then he said again, "Maybe you aren't so dumb!" He continued, "My job would be a cakewalk if it wasn't for…" he paused with a look of despair on his face. "If it wasn't for THEM!"

"I'm seeing it now." I proclaimed, "The enemy uses good tweekers to bring people to their destiny, and to combat the tweekers you play. I went on, "So when it comes to Greble and to Joshua—the enemy won."

"They didn't win yet!" Crampz rebuked emphatically, "Who wins in the end is what really matters. We have other techniques. For example, right now Greble is pretty discouraged due to some things the enemy threw his way."

Risking being called a *dummy* again, I asked, "Wait a minute, what did I hear you say? Why would the enemy want to discourage Greble?" I must have asked a legitimate question because Crampz answered me without his usual sneer.

"It's hard to explain," Crampz said. "Here's where it gets technical. It takes years to get the feel of how the enemy works. They can do things we can't because they have *The Position*. You see, because the enemy already has *The Position*, they have nothing to lose if they lose people. Don't get me wrong, they don't want to lose people, but they don't need large numbers of people in order to keep The Position. If they lose someone, they lose someone. They don't like it, but it doesn't hurt *The Position*. Our goal is to get control of people; their goal is to pave the way for people to become their best, to become what the Maker designed them to be. And sometimes, in order to accomplish this, they allow their victims—or whatever they call their clients—to become discouraged when they get off the track of their destiny. They allow their victim's plans to fail, or their friends to betray them. They allow horrible things to happen to people- things that we would never dream of."

I chirped up, "I don't believe *that!*"

"Well," Crampz admitted, "We wouldn't do it unless we could control them with it. Now with Greble, a major food source from the West just closed, which cut off 75% of the supplies he distributes to the poor. Two months have gone by and Greble has not found a replacement for the supplies."

"What's the enemy's strategy?" I asked.

"I don't know. Who do you think I am, Lassie? I can only ever guess what's happening. My guess is that they're trying to get Greble to find a closer source of supply that is far better than the one back home. What I do know is that the enemy never does something like this without a good purpose in mind. But I know something else, too, that if I can get Greble discouraged enough to quit, he'll be done for, once and for all, and he's almost at that point now.

"Right now Greble feels hopeless. We're replaying those tweekers we played when he was a kid, telling him he is not smart enough to work his way out of this one. We are playing another tweeker that tells him that God has forsaken him. He has done too much wrong and now his humanitarian venture has come to an end.

"And then there's the other woman."

"What?" I exclaimed.

"She works in the medical clinic. Her name is Lisa. She's making Greble feel awfully good about himself. She has nothing but good things to say to Greble, and as low as he feels, it sounds pretty good—especially since Greble's wife is also discouraged and isn't saying a lot of good things these days. We have a team of Wartols working on Greble's wife right this very minute."

Suddenly an alarm sounded. Crampz immediately stopped mid-sentence and quickly slid his seat back to the controls. Frantically he began pushing all sorts of buttons, turning knobs, and carelessly grabbing tweekers. For every one he grabbed, three or four fell on the floor, creating a scene of absolute chaos.

Obviously something serious had just transpired. "What's happening?" I asked.

*"Quiet!"* Crampz screamed at the top of his lungs.

The screen showed Greble sitting on a log by a picturesque stream. He was weeping.

Crampz was throwing tweekers into the player one after the next.

*"You can't quit now. These people need you!"*

"You're just wasting your time. This was the worst thing that could have happened."

*"Be strong. Have faith in God. You came this far with*

49

*God's help, and with help you can overcome this obstacle too."*

"You've tried everything. You're not smart enough to overcome this. Besides, your third-grade teacher was right, you'll never succeed."

*"Your wife needs you now more than ever to be strong. Prevailing here will put new life in your relationship."*

"Lisa makes you feel so good. It's time to start a whole different life without all the pressures, without all the responsibilities. You have done a great job here and helped many people, now it's time to think about yourself and become happy in a new life."

*"Happiness is doing what you are destined to do, and your destiny is right here."*

*"People will help."*

*"There are answers."*

*"Take new strength."*

*"You are a very qualified man."*

I was watching war—right in front of my eyes. One tweeker was from *Scam, Inc.*, the other from the enemy. But then suddenly it was like the enemy's tweekers were the only tweekers being played. Crampz turned up the volume of his tweekers so loud I had to hold my ears. But I perceived that Greble wasn't even hearing Crampz's tweekers. Something was blocking the *Scam, Inc.* tweekers.

As I watched, Greble stood up with a peaceful smile, and walked to a tiny hut where his wife greeted him. He embraced her and began weeping…and then she began weeping. Crampz began screaming "NO! NO!" He pounded the table, and tried a few more tweekers. But it was obvious. Crampz had lost a major battle here. Greble had made a choice. He chose to listen to those whom Crampz called *The Enemy.*

It was like a movie. My eyes welled up with tears of joy while Crampz put his head down pounding the desk in defeat. When the last tweeker ended, everything suddenly quieted in the control room right about the time I let out a jubilant and triumphant *"Yes!"*

At that Crampz lifted up his head slowly. He turned and looked at me. Tears were streaming down my face and a smile was stretching from ear to ear.

"Who are you?" Crampz demanded. "You weren't sent here by *Scam, Inc.*, were you?"

"Uh oh," I said under my breath. I was in trouble now.

# PART TWO: TRUTH PREVAILING

## ☙ A BRIGHTER ROOM ❧

Crampz reached up and pulled a long frayed rope that sounded a piercing alarm. A lighted sign on the wall flashed *Intruder, Intruder!* "You're a spy!" Crampz shouted.

I quickly tried to defend myself but to no avail. A side door opened to the control room and out came three huge Wartols to find out what was going on. They were about twice as tall as Crampz and wider by far. Crampz screamed, pointing to me, "He's a spy! Get him!"

Before they could maneuver around the equipment, I turned and ran out the door through which I had entered. I ran down the tubular corridor, not sure if I was running towards freedom or further into the unknown. My former excitement at Greble's victory was replaced with fear. Where was I? I looked behind me and saw that the Wartols were following me down each curve. The way I ran was differ-

ent than before. The area around me was lit and pulsing, as if it had awakened from sleep. Through the translucent walls I saw massive gray folds of some strange matter. The tube I was in dipped down, and I stumbled and slid through its curving descent. I slid passed a portion of odd, glandular structures against the membrane of the tube. Off to the right I noticed a valve-like portion of the wall and before I could stumble by I thrust my hand into the small opening and pulled myself through. I fell almost straight down, rolling along the steep floor until it curved abruptly to a level plane. As soon as I could get up I saw the first Wartol come tumbling after me. I screamed, "Help! Somebody! Anybody!"

From a doorway just ahead, a tiny creature popped his head out and motioned me to enter. Was this a trick? Who was this other little creature? I needed to find my way out of this place I was in. The thought of undergoing another ordeal such as I had just gone through with Crampz was more than I could handle. In desperation though, I turned and ran into the doorway only to find that I was in another small room with no other way out. The little creature slammed the door shut behind me. Alarmed, I quickly tried to escape before the pursuing creatures caught up to me, but the little creature stood in front of me with a smile and said, "Calm down! It's OK."

"But won't they come in after me?" I asked in panic.

"Are you kidding? They wouldn't dare. You see, we've got *The Position* and they know better than to come into this place."

"You've got *The Position?*" I asked excitedly.

"Why, yes," the creature answered. "Are you familiar with *The Position?*"

"Not really," I replied. "All I know is that you must be the ones who they call *The Enemy.*"

"Right you are," he responded. "But anyways, I welcome you to *Destiny Control: Substation Elvin Greble.*"

"You saved my life. Thanks. But how do you know that I'm not one of them? How did you know to let me in?"

"It really doesn't matter to me who you are or whose side you're on, for you see, we have *The Position.* One of *us* on *their* territory is a major threat to them, but one of *them* on *our* territory, well, at most it's a nuisance. In fact, most of the time *Scam, Inc.* actually helps us succeed in our mission. That's part of what it means to have *The Position*—it means ultimately *we win.*"

I looked around. This control room was brighter than *Scam, Inc.'s* although the equipment in both rooms looked nearly the same. As I drew closer, however, I could see that *Scam, Inc.'s* equipment had been only an inexpensive copy of the technology found in this room. It was obvious that this room had the best equipment available. I noticed that there were multitudes of tweekers, neatly organized, on several shelves, though not nearly as many as in Crampz's chamber.

The little creature put out his hand: "My name is Grimmit. What's yours?"

"Irving MacDonald, but since Irving isn't a very attractive name these days I just go by Mack."

Grimmit immediately chuckled and said, "Sounds like you've been listening to *Scam* tweekers."

Embarrassed, I didn't know what to say to that, but Grimmit broke my silence with a smile and asked, "How can I help you today?"

"Ah…ah…I'm not sure. I didn't ask to come here. I don't think so anyway. But after being with …a…them over there, I guess I'd be interested in what you do. I really have no idea how I got here. I just had an extensive training session with Crampz. Do you know Crampz? You sure I'm safe here?"

"Do I know Crampz?" Grimmit resounded, "I know Crampz better than anyone knows him. In this business it helps to know the enemy, and yes, yes, I assure you, you are safe."

"Hmmm, where would you like me to begin?" Grimmit asked.

"What did you mean when you said that *Scam, Inc.* sometimes helps you succeed in your mission?" I asked.

"Good question," Grimmit stated. Grimmit's response made me feel good, since Crampz had been so crude and insulting.

He continued, "We use far more tactics and strategies than *Scam, Inc.*. They are limited to the same tricks over and over again. Their intent is to destroy people, which they do quite well. But the intent of *Destiny Control* is to help people achieve the destiny for which the Maker designed them. They, over there, operate for their own survival and control. We operate for the Maker's control.

"Tell me more about *The Position*."

57

"It may appear that we at *Destiny Control* have lost far more battles than *Scam, Inc.*—we have, but having *The Position* means we are still winning the war. They may have many notches on their victory belt, but our victories are quality victories. Our victories change hearts. Having *The Position* means the end result is ours—truth and right living will prevail. *Scam, Inc.'s* only hope is to get enough victories that they can totally squelch all of our influence."

"Could they ever do that?" I asked a bit fearfully.

"They *will* never do that, but it is their only hope. They MUST believe that they can prevail. They are doomed if they don't prevail. They have nothing to lose and everything to gain by fighting for *The Position*. That's why Crampz is so intense. If he doesn't get results, he's history.

"They are only able to destroy. Sometimes they destroy by giving people success and sometimes they destroy by helping people fail. They know what many people don't know, that success is not destiny. Success often is the curse of existence.

"One skill we have that they don't have, because we have *The Position,* is the ability to use everything that they do to help people achieve their destiny. When we win a victory against them, they have to come up with a new weapon or strategy. When they send us a mighty blow, we actually use the results of their attack to accomplish our purposes."

"You're not saying that nothing bad can happen to a person, are you?" I asked.

"In one way *yes* and in one way *no*. *No*, meaning that people do make bad choices, and unfortunate things happen to people that cause them much hardship and emotional setbacks. The *yes* part to that answer is nothing bad can happen to a person that can't be used for good and to achieve destiny's purpose."

## ❧ EXAMPLES FROM DESTINY CONTROL ❧

"Let me give you an example. Elvin Greble, whose control room we're in, has a friend, Dan, who is a medical doctor. *Scam, Inc.* tormented Dan all his life. Dan's parents divorced when he was young. After his father left his mother, he never returned to see Dan. His mother abused alcohol. Dan blamed himself for his parent's breakup. He would often say that his life was *worthless mud. Scam, Inc.* rejoiced in what they had done to Dan. But we knew, here at *Destiny Control*, that Dan was just fitting nicely into the Maker's plan.

We sent some of our people to encourage Dan, and to take him under their wings. One of those was a soccer coach that had a great love for Dan and saw potential in him. Another was a science teacher that worked overtime with Dan and helped him discover his interest in the medical field. Dan made some right choices along the way. He decided that he wanted to mentor those who grew up like him.

As he grew up, instead of being a victim of *Scam, Inc.*, as they expected, he became an archenemy of *Scam, Inc.* He was constantly encouraging people *with the sensitivity that he had learned through his own unfortunate circumstances in life*—those predominantly created by *Scam, Inc.*

We have used Dan to encourage thousands and thousands of people, and we have only one organization to thank for that: *Scam, Inc.* Here at *Destiny Control,* we just kept on playing back the tweekers of the few people who saw Dan's potential."

"Amazing!" I exclaimed. "How do you stay secret?"

"Secret?" Grimmit exclaimed. "We don't have to stay secret. *Scam, Inc.*? They have to stay secret. Once people perceive what is going on in their mind, they can learn how to resist *Scam, Inc.'s* nasty lies. Here we speak nothing but truth, and with truth there is nothing to hide. We actually hope people find out about us, because then they will understand the power of having *The Position*—but they must find us on their own, for this is the test of their heart."

"I get it," I said. "When people find out about you, they are glad and will listen to you instead of *Scam, Inc.*"

"I didn't say that," Grimmit clarified. "Much of what we have to say to people is truth, but it is difficult truth— truth that people don't necessarily want to hear. I wish people always wanted to hear the truth, but sadly, many people reject the truth because of the pain that the truth often causes. Many people are much more attached to *Scam, Inc.*

"We don't calculate our success by numbers, like *Scam, Inc.* does. If we wanted numbers we wouldn't expose people to the *difficult truth*, and also, we would make our operation more obvious to people. But then we would only save people on the outside, and not on the inside. When people are just changed on the outside they become a greater target for *Scam, Inc.*

"I'll tell you a true story about a young person named David who found out about *Scam, Inc*. He raced dirt bikes for a hobby. Several times he wrecked, or had injuries in races. David misinterpreted some things that some people he respected said about the wrecks, like *perhaps God was teaching him a lesson through his wrecks*. David assumed that he was always destined to wreck in races. Every time he got to the starting line, *Scam, Inc*. played the fearful tweekers David had recorded himself, and David feared wrecking again. One day David realized, through the help of his parents, that this fear was nothing but a lie that had no root in truth. David chose to quit listening to those tweekers anymore and was set free to enjoy racing, and to race safely. Amazingly, he didn't have any more wrecks."

"Utterly amazing!" I exclaimed, "Crampz told me some of the tweekers he uses the most. Would you mind telling me some of the tweekers you use the most."

"Not at all," Grimmit replied. "Here are just a few of the millions we use:

*'You are a valuable person.'*

*'You are worthy to be loved.'*

*'Failure is just a step toward success.'*

*'You are valuable for who you are, not for what you do.'*

*'You don't have to do great things to be important.'*

*'What people think doesn't really matter, only what God thinks matters.'*

*'You CAN follow your dreams.'*

*'Serious mistakes don't disqualify you from being forgiven.'*

*'Doing what is right is better than doing what feels good or doing what works.'*
*'You are not stupid.'*
*'Giving always returns with a greater blessing.'*
*'Outward image is not valuable to your true destiny.'*
*'A degree of pain accompanies almost all good choices.'"*

## ❧ COURAGE, TRUTH AND LANCE ❧

Grimmit continued, "Tweekers, all kinds of tweekers, from all kinds of sources, play in people's minds all the time. Tweekers keep people happy, tweekers keep people sad, tweekers keep people in fear, and tweekers make people courageous; tweekers keep people living up to someone else's expectation for their whole life, tweekers set people free to become who they were meant to be. Everyone's mind plays back tweekers— either lies or truth, either constructive or destructive. They are either a blessing in the long run or a curse forever.

"In this world there are a multitude of sources for lies; the sources of truth are few. Lies outnumber statements of truth in this world 500 to 1. That is why we must persist in our quest to change people's hearts. To change their outward behavior is much easier than changing their heart. A changed heart is one that has cleansed itself from the tweekers that lie and oppress."

"Grimmit," I said. "What makes the difference between those who find their destiny and those who don't?"

"Hummm," Grimmit responded. "That's a big question. To answer that let me give you an example from someone you've probably heard about. His name is Lance Armstrong. Lance was a rich, world-class athlete, one of the top bike riders in the world, headed toward being the best, that is until Lance got cancer.

"Scam, Inc. attacked him. His first thought when he found out that he had cancer was, 'I'll never race again!' During chemotherapy Lance lost most of his muscle strength. It was quite discouraging for him, to say the least. Lance never knew his father, but his mother was his most loyal supporter. Lance also had some incredible friends that made some awesome tweekers.

"Well, the short of it is that Lance came back, after cancer, chemo and brain surgery, to win the most grueling sporting event on earth, the *Tour de France*, a 2,290 mile road race. Lance said, 'Cancer was the best thing that ever happened to me.' Not only did he win it once, he won it seven times, and maybe more, I stopped counting."

"I bet you were playing tweekers all the time in his mind," I said.

"Nonsense!" Grimmit replied. "When there are friends and family that encourage like Lance's did, there's not much we have to do. We simply, time-to-time, replay some of those tweekers of truth and courage. But there is another issue; again it is the issue of the heart. Some people have a heart of courage. They are fertile ground for what *Destiny Control* has to offer. There are some people, though, who lack courage. They despise pain and sacrifice and don't really want truth. There is little anyone can do for a person who doesn't want to change.

"Indeed, it doesn't really matter how much someone has failed in his or her life or how much they believe they have messed up their destiny. If their heart is willing to receive truth and embrace courage faith and the pain of self-sacrifice they can make their life worthwhile and achieve a worthwhile destiny."

"Well, Grimmit, Crampz told me what he believed to be the greatest lie on the face of the earth: *sticks and stones will break my bones but words will never hurt me*. What would you say is the greatest truth?"

"What a question! Depends what category we're talking about, but one of the greatest truths ever spoken was popularized through a TV commercial advertising milk. It goes like this: *"Today is the first day of the rest of your life."*

Suddenly, just like in Control Room #1, a loud, alarm sounded.

## ✎✒ WAR FROM THE OTHER SIDE ✒✎

Grimmit immediately turned from me and responded to the screen and controls. In a second or two Greble was on screen. He was in the yard of the medical clinic with Lisa, the warm-natured lady friend Crampz told me about. It was obvious that Lisa was interested in capturing Greble's heart. First she small-talked with him and then she focused in on Greble's hurting heart. Wow, did she pour on the encouragement and the concern! She appeared to be so loving and innocent.

Then, Scam, Inc. started working. Thoughts—tweekers—began pouring into his mind.

*Here's your chance to take care of yourself.*

*Don't waste the rest of your life fighting to see something happen that may not happen.*

*Your mission to these people is over. Now focus on personal happiness.*

*Lisa is the kind of companion that would always make you happy.*

I anxiously watched Grimmit just sitting there watching. What was he doing? Or what was he NOT doing? He wasn't putting in any tweekers to counteract Crampz. I understood that Grimmit told people truth, but to let Greble alone at a time such as this seemed positively cruel. I couldn't contain myself and snapped at Grimmit, "What are you doing? Why aren't you helping the guy? He's obviously no Lance Armstrong."

Grimmit just looked at me. He said nothing and went back to viewing the screen. Then he calmly replied to my outburst: "This is the true test of Greble's heart. He is fully capable of combating Crampz on his own. We have given him all he needs. Now his heart must be tested."

"But if he fails?" I questioned.

Grimmit looked at me and without a sound answered me with his eyes. I knew he was saying, "If he fails, he fails."

I watched anxiously to see if Greble would pass the test. I wanted to scream, *Come on Greble!*

"This woman is wonderful," thought Greble.

"Who was that?" I asked. "Was that Crampz or Greble?"

Grimmit answered, "That, my friend, was not Crampz."

My heart sank, but then came the thought, "But I can't sacrifice the good thing I have for a cheap experience. I will no longer play with this enticement. I am more valuable than to fall for a cheap affair."

"Did you do that, Grimmit, or was that Greble's original thought, too?"

"That was Greble."

As we watched, Greble politely told Lisa that he must be running along. He smiled and walked out of the yard.

"Good boy, Greb!" I shouted.

Grimmit looked at me with a smile, "Well, well, we don't need to worry about Greble any more. He just won a major victory today that strengthened his heart against anything *Scam, Inc.* could ever send his way. After today, Crampz may find himself back at *Warner Brothers* working with cartoons. In fact," Grimmit laughed, "He may even get the part of a villain chasing the good guy who never loses. You know, the guys who run off cliffs and have heavy boulders fall on their head, and bombs blow up in their faces." Grimmit stopped and keeled over with a big belly laugh just imagining Crampz playing such a ridiculous part. He was laughing so hard that I couldn't help laughing myself. It had to be three or four minutes before we could contain ourselves again.

Finally, as the laughter subsided, Grimmit stood from his chair and looked at me. With a smile still lurking around the corners of his mouth, he said, "It has been a pleasure. I hope that I have helped you."

"More than you know," I responded.

I knew it was time to go home, but I didn't know where to go. Grimmit sensed my dilemma and asked, "Do you need someone to show you the way out?"

"Yes," I said.

We exited the door behind me and walked down the long, circular corridor. Grimmit pointed and said, "Just go that way and you'll be OK."

I looked down the passageway and saw that it was pitch black. I turned to Grimmit to ask for more precise directions, but to my surprise, he was gone. Not only was *he* gone, but as I turned back to the direction in which Grimmit had pointed, I saw that I was no longer in the dark hallway. I walked forward only to find myself in the same dense fog that had gotten me here in the first place. In just a few short moments, I noticed the fog begin to lift. I immediately saw where I was, and briskly continued my walk back to my home.

# PART THREE: PROCESSING THE STRANGE INCIDENT

The next few days, weeks, and months were interesting for a couple of reasons. For one, I began to detect and point out *Scam, Inc.* tweekers that were playing in the mind of those who came to me for wisdom. I began seeing people set free from guilt, shame, defeat, sexual abuse, insecurity, fears, worries, selfishness, boredom, depression and more—all because they destroyed the power of those lying *Scam, Inc.* tweekers.

But more than that, I became aware of tweekers that were playing in my own mind that were keeping me from experiencing the fullness of joy and from reaching my destiny. These I didn't catch immediately once I was home. I sort of set an ambush on my mind to catch these despicable tweekers as soon as they played.

In two weeks I logged two full pages of lies that played over and over again in my mind. They were replays of things my peers had said to me, things my parents had told me, things authorities had told me, and lots of self-talk tweekers. The more tweekers I caught the more I became free…and fulfilled. In those next few months I changed for the good more than I ever changed in my life. I started filling my mind with good thoughts: thoughts of truth, faith, confidence, love and victory. I even came up with my own library of tweekers that I would repeat to myself every day. These tweekers reminded me to fight, to look on the bright side of life, to discipline myself and to forgive my past.

## ☙ THE MOST MAGNIFICENT MESSAGE ❧

But I *must* tell you about the most magnificent message I received after my experience. As I progressed in my freedom from lying tweekers, I sensed pieces of a tweeker that was trying to come through to my heart. I kept hearing the word *comeback*. The message though, was like trying to understand someone who was shouting an important message to me from a hill a long mile away—I was catching only a few unconnected words.

One day I decided to set myself to understand what was happening in my mind and thus I retreated to a solitary place by a mellow stream behind my house, under a weeping willow tree. I cleared my mind of the hustle of life and basked in the peace of nature. It wasn't long till the tweeker, or the message, whatever you want to call it, came through to my heart loud and clear.

It was Destiny Control saying, "Make a comeback! You can do it! Today is the first day of the rest of your life!"

"That's it!" I shouted. I can make a comeback! I hadn't lost any time, for I am wiser today because of my journey in life, and even because of my failures. I decided: *I will make the best of my life from now on.*

You see, I have failed several times in my life in different areas—things much more serious than the death of Winston the frog. I didn't seem to have the day-to-day victories and successes in my life that I saw in other people that I admired. I would rarely take the initiative to offer advice to people who were struggling in life simply because I felt unworthy. Yet people would still come to me to seek my advice. What did they see in me? They knew of my failures, yet somehow it didn't matter to those who came.

Now I understand. I don't have as many victories as some others, but I could see that many of the successes I did have were quality victories. I know now that life is not necessarily a series of day-to-day encounters with success, but sometimes it may only be five golden victories in our life—or perhaps just three, *or maybe only one*, that makes our whole life worthwhile to have lived. It may be that I, or you, will inspire or influence one person by our life who will change the world for good, something we may die never having known. Could it really be that some people are put here on earth by the Maker for just one such solitary success? I believe so.

So friend, take heart, stand up, say no to *Scam, Inc.*, those of you who have fallen victim to your own failures. Life awaits you, no matter your age. Your purpose is not yet fulfilled. Make a comeback.

In the days and months that followed my bizarre expe-

YOU'VE BEEN TWEEKED!

71

rience, my eyes were opened more and more, day by day to the life-crushing oppression people endure because of the vicious lies they subconsciously believe. I saw people gripped by poverty, others lonely, some striving every day just to preserve a dry morsel of happiness…and behind it all are the tweekers—the lies that play incessantly in their minds. Yet I also perceived that their road to victory is ever so attainable. Oh, if I could only change the way they think. But they must do that themselves. I can only present them with the truth I now see and know.

Friend, would you like to get free? Perhaps you have secret tweekers hidden in your subconscious that are influencing you to make inadequate choices. Take some time to listen. Is Scam, Inc. playing those lies that seem so true, but keep you oppressed and unhappy? Go out by the weeping willow tree and write down all the negative tweekers that control you. It is time to replace those tweekers with the tweekers of *Destiny Control. Destiny Control* believes in you, and believes that no matter what you've done in your life or no matter how many mistakes you have made, that you can exit this life having made a positive mark on humanity, and having reached your true purpose in God.

And I guess that's where it all comes together—God's will for your life. I hope you can see that beyond *Destiny Control* there is someone who is rooting for you and wants to take control of your life—and that is God. Go for it. You can do it. I promise. He'll make your life worthwhile. I wish you the best.

*Yours truly,*
IRVING

# PART FOUR: STUDY & DISCUSSION GUIDE

1. While reading *You've Been Tweeked*, did you become aware of any tweekers that play in your mind? Describe them. Are they from *Scam, Inc.* or *Destiny Control*?

2. Write down the areas in your life you struggle with such as finances, relationships, employment, addictive behaviors, self-hate, hatred toward parents, resentment, inability to make anything succeed, and so forth. This will give you an indication where to search for negative tweekers.

3. Take the list of common tweekers from Crampz's explanation, which of the following might apply the most to you?

- You're a bad girl (or boy)
- You're too ugly to be important
- Everything you do is sloppy

- If people see who you really are they won't like you
- Don't try this or that because you'll fail
- You aren't good enough to make God happy with you
- You need to have a little fun before you get serious in life
- No matter how hard you try, you'll never be as good as your sister
- If you fail at this you'll be a nobody
- You have to look good and be in shape to be socially acceptable
- Making money is the only way to get ahead
- You'll never be rich and successful
- You don't have the ability to do this
- If you put your fellow workers down, you'll get ahead

Add to this list, if you can, from your personal experience, and from the list you made first.

**Take each tweeker that plays in your mind and ask:**
- Does this tweeker help me or hinder me?
- Is it true or false?
- What true fact will combat this lie?
- Did this tweeker come from my parents, my friends, my self-talk, my spiritual leader, a teacher, or someone else?

**Tweeker exercise #1**: Think for a minute about the

kind of car you drive, the kind of clothing you own, the amount in your savings account. When the desire comes to improve these things what are some of the thoughts that come to your mind?

Examples: I am not worthy of nice things; I need nice things to be happy and gain the respect of others; I can't afford to buy nicer things; it is better to have less than to have more.

**Tweeker exercise #2**: Think about the depth of your best relationship. When the desire comes to improve that relationship, or a relationship you want to be better, what thoughts come to mind?

Evaluate the above thoughts. Are they bless-ings or hindrances? Are they true or are they lies?

• **Fear**: List tweekers that play in your mind that make you fearful. Think about relationships, circumstances, money, business, spiritual things, the future, your physical condition.

• **Insecurity**: List tweekers that play in your mind that make you insecure in various settings. For example, what goes through your mind when you walk into a room full of people you don't know? How about when you walk into a room full of people you do know?

• **Dreams and visions**: List tweekers that play in your mind that help you or hinder you from accomplishing your dreams in life. For example, are you afraid to takes risks in order to stretch your influence? Or do you stay in safe zones?

• **Wounds and hurts**: List tweekers that play in your mind that cause you to avoid pain. Knowing that the best things in life come with pain, sacrifice and suffering, how can you train your mind to embrace necessary and positive pain?

• **Evaluate the above tweekers**: Are these tweekers Scam, Inc. or Destiny Control? How can you combat any negative, crippling thoughts and mentalities that keep you from becoming your best?

• Now that you've discovered the control rooms in your mind and exposed the lies, write down how you are going to be different from now on. What will change in your life? After you do this, write down a list of other people you know that are victims of negative tweekers. Beside their name, write down how you can help them! Don't be afraid. You were rescued, now go rescue others. Believe me, *Someone* will be helping you!

# GETTING FREE AT THE ROOT

*Seminar*

## ❧ MAXIMIZING YOUR DESTINY ❧

Bruce and Ruthie Lengeman are available to teach Getting Free At the Root at your church, self-help group, marriage conference or addiction recovery group. You've Been Tweeked! is a story that exposes the central reason why some people fail and others succeed; Getting Free At the Root takes up where You've Been Tweeked! ends. It is a challenging and educational seminar that teaches you how get free in your core belief system. The seminar is fun and practical—designed to impact your life from the inside out. You can contact Bruce Lengeman at:

*Bruce@leadershipfoundation.net.*

TATE PUBLISHING & *Enterprises*

Tate Publishing is commited to excellence in the publishing industry. Our staff of hightly trained professionals, including editors, graphic designers, and marketing personnel, work together to produce the very finest books available. The company reflects the philosophy established by the founders, based on Psalms 68:11,

"THE LORD GAVE THE WORD AND GREAT WAS THE COMPANY
OF THOSE WHO PUBLISHED IT."

If you would like further information, please call
1.888.361.9473
or visit our website
www.tatepublishing.com

TATE PUBLISHING & *Enterprises*, LLC
127 E. Trade Center Terrace
Mustang, Oklahoma 73064 USA